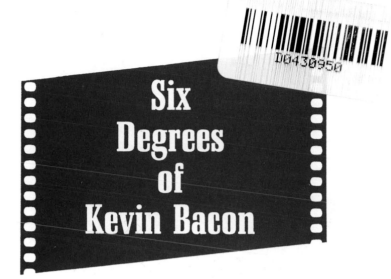

Six
Degrees
of
Kevin Bacon

Six
Degrees
of
Kevin Bacon

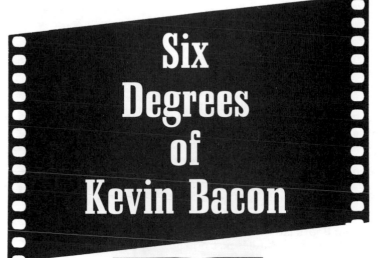

CRAIG FASS, MIKE GINELLI, AND BRIAN TURTLE

A PLUME BOOK

PLUME
Published by the Penguin Group
Penguin Books USA Inc., 375 Hudson Street, New York
New York 10014, U.S.A.
Penguin Books Ltd, 27 Wrights Lane, London W8 5TZ, England
Penguin Books Australia Ltd, Ringwood, Victoria, Australia
Penguin Books Canada Ltd, 10 Alcorn Avenue, Toronto, Ontario,
Canada M4V 3B2
Penguin Books (N.Z.) Ltd, 182–190 Wairau Road, Auckland 10,
New Zealand

Penguin Books Ltd, Registered Offices:
Harmondsworth, Middlesex, England

First published by Plume, an imprint of Dutton Signet,
a division of Penguin Books USA Inc.

First Printing, September, 1996
10   9   8   7   6   5

Copyright © GinzFassTurtle, LLC, 1996
Introduction copyright © Kevin Bacon, 1996
Photos courtesy of Photofest
All rights reserved

Library of Congress Cataloging-in-Publication Data is available.

ISBN: 0-452-27844-9

Printed in the United States of America
Set in Univers
Designed by Stanley Drate & Ellen Gleeson/Folio Graphics Co. Inc.

BOOKS ARE AVAILABLE AT QUANTITY DISCOUNTS WHEN USED TO PROMOTE
PRODUCTS OR SERVICES. FOR INFORMATION PLEASE WRITE TO PREMIUM MARKETING
DIVISION, PENGUIN BOOKS USA INC., 375 HUDSON STREET, NEW YORK, NY 10014.

Dedicated to
Kevin Bacon and Pat Vogt

ACKNOWLEDGMENTS

Thanks to everyone who helped contribute to the making of this game and this book. Thanks to the Fass family, the Ginelli family, and the Turtle family. Thanks to Albright College for giving us nothing better to do, and thanks to the brothers at Zeta Omega Epsilon. Thanks to Jon Stewart, Stuart Bailey, and Eileen Katz for putting us on the show and letting us meet Kevin Bacon. And thanks to Howard Stern and Gary Dell'Abate for everything. We'd also like to thank Sean Casey, our attorney; Todd Keithley, our editor; and Dan Strone, our literary agent.

Specifically, we'd each like to thank the following people:

BRIAN: Marge, Jack, and Kristen Turtle; Christi Tucci; and everyone at Aerotek. Also Dawgs, Hart, Shane, Medland, Johnny, and Jaquinto.

MIKE: John and Beverly Ginelli; John Tara and Alyssa Ginelli; members of Q-Law Rugby Team; G. Weiss; Darn and Nuke; Chad Levant; and Javier Garguillo.

Also in memory of Jeanne Montesano, who gave me my love of movies, and Orlando Ginelli, who gave me a zest for life.

CRAIG: I'd like to thank Wolf, Death, and Wolf Jr.; Stacy; Joanne and her family; Loop; Mike and his family; Dawgs; Sek; and Cheryl.

And of course, thanks to Kevin Bacon.

CONTENTS

Introduction: A Few Words from Kevin Bacon   **11**
How We Got Our Start   **13**
Kevin Bacon: A Filmography   **21**

PART I • THE BASIC BACON

Missing Links   **33**
Kevins to Kevin   **34**
The Baldwin Family Tree   **37**
Bridges to Bacon   **40**
Meatheads and Bacon   **42**
Bacon and Legs   **46**
Singing to Bacon   **49**
Rapping to Bacon   **53**
Black and White   **56**

PART II • TELEVISION

Our Rules   61
Seinfeld   62
The Facts of Life   64
TV Hosts   66

PART III • THE UNUSUAL BACON

Dancing to *Footloose*   71
Pigskins to Bacon   74
The Animal Kingdom   76
Bringing Home the Bacon   79
Superbacon   81
Close Encounters with Kevin   84
Driving Mr. Bacon   87
Monsters, not including those huge sand worms
   from *Tremors*   89
Dynamic Duos   91

PART IV • THE ANSWERS

Introduction:
A Few Words from
Kevin Bacon

O.K., I admit it. When I first heard about the game, I was less than thrilled. Maybe it was because I was told it was a drinking game sweeping across college campuses, and I thought, oh great, I'll be accused of contributing to teenage alcoholism. I pictured myself doing public service announcements saying, "Just say no to the Kevin Bacon game."

Maybe it was the fact that I had been working so hard to legitimize my career, to be respected as an actor, to be taken seriously. And now the last twenty years of my life had become a game, or as I perceived it, a joke at my expense.

Maybe I was having a low self-esteem day.

All that changed when I met Craig, Brian, and Mike or, as Jon Stewart called them, "The Kevin Bacon Guys." I realized that these guys actually liked my movies, actually did respect me, and were very good at the game (even though I think I stumped them with Larry Storch).

Over time, as the popularity of the game increased, I realized I was developing a fondness for it, although I'm not very good at it, and my playing is by definition cheating.

It's a hard thing for people to understand, but, to survive an acting career, you have to put up with a lot of rejection. Even as lucky as I have been, there will always be a list of guys who get parts before I do, get more press, better reviews, and make a lot more money than I do. But, hey, I'm the only one with a game! And, I have to admit, I dig that. I once read somewhere that the game could be played with Arnold Schwarzenegger and it bugged me. I thought, "Hey, put your terminator back in your pocket big man, this is *my game!*"

Everywhere I go, folks ask me about it, and my only explanation is that the world was probably getting sick of "Twenty Questions."

I just had the opportunity to work with four very talented teenage actors in "Sleepers," and I realized that I was laying the groundwork for playing long after I am six feet under.

So, I'll keep acting. You keep playing. But don't forget to spend some of that leisure time going to the movies or I'll be out of a job.

KEVIN BACON
Cleveland
August 1996

How We Got Our Start

The three of us came up with this game late one night at college. An advertisement for Kevin Bacon's most recent movie, *The Air Up There,* was playing on TV. Somehow it occurred to us that Kevin Bacon had been in so many different types of movies, you could connect a lot of unlikely people together through his work.

Well, that idea took off. We found we could actually get *anybody* back to Kevin Bacon in a few steps. There could only be one explanation—Kevin Bacon was at the center of the entertainment universe.

With that in mind, we wrote a completely over-the-top letter to the *Jon Stewart Show.*

Mardi Montgomery
MTV 1775 Broadway
Jon Stewart Show
January 15, 1994

It started as a joke, a game, if you will. The weather was cold and the three of us were inside keeping ourselves warm with a bottle of Southern Comfort. The television was on, but no one was watching—no one was watching until one man's name was mentioned. That name was Kevin Bacon; the commercial was for his new movie, *The Air Up There.* Kevin Bacon, two words that often remind us of such movies as *Footloose* or *He Said, She Said.* Innocent enough, that name changed our lives, and became the center of much conversation here at Albright College.

Being Connoisseurs of the Silver Screen (the proclaimed ''Grand Wizards of Movie Trivia''), the three of us slowly began to realize that Kevin Bacon was the center of the entertainment universe. The idea was simple enough: Name an actor or actress, and we can link him or her to Kevin Bacon through celebrities in other movies or TV shows. This seed, however, began to blossom, and now the three of us can't go five minutes without linking a new actor or actress to Mr. Bacon. As time passes, we grow stronger—maybe too strong! We are sure that we are not only speaking for ourselves when we say it can be scary. Like the time when we linked Thurston Howell III, Bruce Lee, or Gary Coleman to Kevin

Bacon. We are three men on a mission. Our mission is to prove to the Jon Stewart audience, nay, the world, that Bacon is God. Furthermore, we believe that if given the opportunity to demonstrate our unusual talent to you, we will captivate the audience of the *Jon Stewart Show* as we have done to our campus, and you also will see Kevin Bacon in a new light.

Please do not hesitate to call us if you come across any questions or if you want a demonstration. 1-215-555-5555, ask for Craig. We are looking forward to hearing from you.

Sincerely yours,

Craig Fass
Brian Turtle
Mike Ginelli

The letter was crazy, but it worked. The *Jon Stewart Show* gave us a call, a guy named Stuart Bailey, and asked us to demonstrate Six Degrees of Kevin Bacon. By the end of the call he had us on a speaker phone with eight people, and they were all throwing names at us left and right. From that, we got invited to the real thing.

Upon our arrival at the *Jon Stewart Show* we were treated like celebrities. Well, maybe not celebrities . . . more like circus attractions. The entire studio wanted to meet us, and they drilled us nonstop. They treated us as if we were triplets who felt each other's pain. We were separated and spread around so that everyone would have a shot. Some people even followed us into the bathrooms and hounded us at the urinals.

We did get a green room, given on one condition: when Dennis Leary showed up, we had to leave. The green room was a pretty nice place to hang out, and they had a platter of fruit on the counter, which we devoured. We were pretty embarrassed when Dennis Leary walked in and found that three guys talking about Kevin Bacon had eaten all his food.

We met Jon briefly before the show. Jon treated us like we were part of the family—the part of the family that you keep at a distance. We were put on the back left corner of the stage. When our segment came, we performed well. Jon threw us some names, the audience had a few, and even Dennis Leary got in on the act. At the end of it a woman came running up and gave us a great big hug. It was Eileen Katz, the executive producer of the show. Amazingly, she'd loved the game! At that moment we realized that this Kevin Bacon thing might actually catch on.

In January 1995, Craig and Mike were on Maui studying humpback whales, and got a surprising phone call. Somehow the *Jon Stewart Show* had gotten a hold of the lab's number. Kevin Bacon was booked to promote *Murder in the First* the following week, and they wanted us to be on with him.

All three of us made it to New York, nervous as hell. We were actually going to meet Kevin Bacon. It happened sooner than we thought it would. Before the show they had us waiting in a hallway, and the man we'd spent months of our lives talking about walked by. He stopped, looked at us, and said, "So, you're the guys." Brian said, "Yeah." Our big moment, and all we could come up with was "Yeah." It was a disaster.

Lucky for us, that was the most awkward part of the day. We taped the show, and all went smoothly. It was mostly focused on Kevin Bacon's new movie; we didn't show our stuff much. The day ended, and so did our fifteen minutes of fame. Going into it, Kevin was a little iffy about the game, but he warmed up to it, or at least it seemed like he did. When we were on the Howard Stern show, he even called in. That made the three of us feel great.

And that's how we got our start. Now there are a lot of

people around the country playing Six Degrees of Kevin Bacon. Hopefully all those people will find something funny in this book—a better connection to Kevin Bacon, a new variation on the game, even a movie they didn't realize he was in.

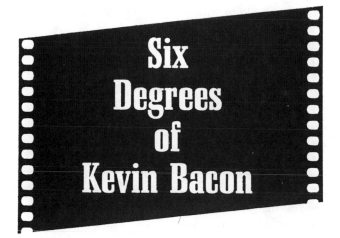

1978	■	National Lampoon's Animal House
1979	■	Starting Over
1980	■	Friday the 13th
1980	■	Hero at Large
1981	■	Only When I Laugh
1982	■	Diner
1982	■	Forty Deuces
1983	■	Enormous Changes at the Last Minute
1984	■	Footloose
1986	■	Quicksilver
1987	■	White Water Summer
1987	■	End of the Line
1987	■	Planes, Trains, and Automobiles (cameo)
1988	■	She's Having a Baby
1989	■	Criminal Law
1989	■	The Big Picture
1990	■	Tremors
1990	■	Flatliners
1991	■	He Said, She Said
1991	■	Queens Logic
1991	■	Pyrates
1991	■	JFK
1992	■	A Few Good Men
1994	■	The Air Up There
1994	■	The River Wild
1995	■	Murder in the First
1995	■	Balto (voice of)
1995	■	Apollo 13
1996	■	Sleepers
1997	■	Picture Perfect
1997	■	Telling Lies in America
1997	■	Digging to China

Kevin Bacon
A FILMOGRAPHY

On July 8, 1958, in the city of Philadelphia, the center of the entertainment universe was born. Twenty years later, Kevin Bacon appeared in his first movie, and the heavens aligned in such a way that everyone could be connected to him through six actor-to-actor links or less.

1978	*Animal House*

That first big break was *Animal House.* Unfortunately, Kevin had only five minutes of air time, he had to wear a beanie, he got hit by the leader of the geek fraternity, and he had to say, "Thank you, sir. May I have another?" But it got the ball rolling. Considering he was a first-time actor who'd been given the chance to get into a great movie like *Animal House,* it was probably worth it. You have to start on the bottom rung. A lot of actors wouldn't want to take that risk, but he got right in there.

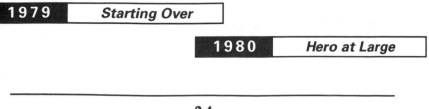

1979	*Starting Over*

1980	*Hero at Large*

1980   *Friday the 13th*

The next major appearance he had was in *Friday the 13th*. The unfortunate thing about being in the original *Friday the 13th* is that you get killed by the mother, and not by Jason. Actually, if Kevin would have been paying more attention, Jason never would have drowned in Crystal Lake, and then he never would have come back and killed all those other people. In a way, you could say Kevin Bacon's responsible for a whole lot of deaths. In a way.

1981   *Only When I Laugh*

1982   *Diner*

Diner is a truly unforgettable movie. He's excellent in that movie, he's really hitting his stride. It's chock full of other great actors, too. Playing the game, a connection through an actor in *Diner* feels so much better than one through *JFK* or *A Few Good Men*.

1983   *Enormous Changes at the Last Minute*

1984   *Footloose*

Footloose. In many respects it's a tearjerker—not that it's sad, really, but that it's so inspiring. We consider this the quintessential Kevin Bacon film; it's where he stood up and said, "I'm Kevin Bacon, hear me roar."

For all three of us, *Footloose* was the first Kevin Bacon movie we saw in the theaters. It was 1984.

Brian: I was going to see *Splash* and it was sold out, so I got stuck seeing *Footloose.* But by the end of the film I said, "Who is this guy? He's great!" The finale in the chapel still gives me goose bumps, when John Lithgow's giving a speech and then Kevin Bacon breaks in and talks about dancing and music and free spirits. "Let them dance!"

Mike: When I saw it, my brother and I thought it was going to be a breakdancing movie. It was a huge disappointment when we realized our mistake, but then, by the end of the movie, we loved it. It was even better than breakdancing. I'll take Kevin Bacon over Ozone, Turbo, and Special K any day.

Craig: When you wonder which Kevin Bacon character would be the best one—if they were all in the same movie and had to fight in a battle royale—you figure it's probably the guy in *Footloose.* It's true Bacon killed a man with a spoon in *Murder in the First,* and that he had the ability to generate fire in *Pyrates* . . . but in *Footloose* he stands up for justice and humanity and what he believes in.

A classic role in *Footloose* is the kid played by Christopher Penn. How great is it when Kevin Bacon's trying to teach him how to dance, out on that country road, while "Let's Hear It for the Boy" is playing? Another great Christopher Penn scene is when he's going through the hallways of the school, and you see him bopping up and down with his headphones on. Playing the game, we try to connect through Christopher Penn whenever possible.

1986   *Quicksilver*

Bacon plays the best bicycle courier ever in *Quicksilver*. He plays a guy who gives up the stock market, who pretty much has a breakdown, leaves it all behind and goes out to make it on his own, in his own way. His race against Laurence Fishburne is one of the most grueling scenes in movie history by far. The look on his face when he's riding his bike up the hill—you feel the pain when you watch that. The thing about *Quicksilver* is that it's not the first movie you think of when you think of Kevin Bacon. That's what makes it a preferred movie to play the game through.

Bacon's basically been a good guy up to this point, except for the fact that he caused all those people to die at Crystal Lake in *Friday the 13th*. But then you get to *White Water Summer*. He comes out of his good-guy shell and gets a little crazy here, playing a deranged camp counselor.

1987   *White Water Summer* aka *Rites of Summer*

The weird thing about *White Water Summer* is that some people call it *Rites of Summer*. Who knows why it has two names, but it's definitely strange. It didn't help the movie much. This may be the only movie ever filmed with two titles.

1987   *Planes, Trains & Automobiles*

You probably missed Kevin Bacon in *Planes, Trains & Automobiles.* Similar to *Animal House,* most people don't know Kevin Bacon's in this movie. They've seen these movies a hundred times, and never realized who was in some of the smaller roles. We hear "Kevin Bacon wasn't in that!" constantly, but he was.

So who is he? He's the guy who snags the cab from Steve Martin. Quick scene—dirty move. Some would say it's a great move, knowing how tough it is to get a cab—it's every man for himself in that situation. It was probably all his training in previous movies that made him so fast. All the footwork, jumping into those crowds and dancing in the hallways in *Footloose,* and the pedalling in *Quicksilver*—it all paid off. The quicker man gets the cab. They're sprinting something like three blocks to get into the taxi. The only person in the movies who might be faster is Carl Lewis, who's in *Speed Zone.* He's only got a cameo: he runs up to a car, hands the driver something, and then runs away. He's pretty fast.

1987	End of the Line

1988	She's Having a Baby

The next Kevin Bacon movie we know anything about is *She's Having a Baby,* which was a 1988 film. The female lead is Elizabeth McGovern. The interesting thing about the film is the montage editing, as opposed to the usual mise-en-scène. (Maybe we should send a copy of this book to our college film professor.) Anyway, the best thing about the movie is that he's in it.

It's too bad they didn't have him dancing in *She's Having a Baby.* Like John Travolta, they should try to squeeze some dancing into anything Kevin Bacon is in. Every movie should have a scene in a hall or on a road, where Kevin Bacon does a little *Footloose* move at some point.

Maybe he jumps up at the end of the movie—he could do a jump at the end of *Murder in the First,* right after he says "I won!" Kick the feet together, freeze frame, and roll credits.

1989 — *Criminal Law*

Criminal Law is an awesome, awesome movie. What a change for him. Gary Oldman, who is an incredible actor in his own right, is also in this film. Going into it, knowing the movie's premise, you think Gary Oldman will play the nut, and you're surprised when it turns out to be Kevin Bacon. But after seeing it, you realize what a great choice Kevin was, and what a smart move it was to cast him in that role.

1989 — *The Big Picture*

Next comes *The Big Picture,* a film about the underbelly of Hollywood. It's a good movie. Everyone's in it. John Cleese has a cameo. Teri Hatcher is in it. There are some really funny parts, like Martin Short's famous line: "I don't know you, I've never seen your work, but I think you're very talented!" Kevin Bacon also delivers a great line while making grilled cheese sandwiches, when he says something like, "The secret is that I take the plastic wrappers off *before* I grill them."

1990 — *Tremors*

Now, *Tremors* is a real cult classic. There was a sequel, *Tremors II,* but it didn't have Kevin Bacon in it. It may have gone straight to video. If you can't get Bacon, forget the theatrical release. There's also a small part in film history worth mentioning here: that classic scene in *Mall Rats,* at the opening of the movie, where you can see a *Tremors* poster in the guy's room. Anyway, if you can get to Kevin Bacon through *Tremors,* you can really play the game.

1990   Flatliners

The same year that *Tremors* came out, Kevin was also in *Flatliners*. It's a great movie. They're med school students who experiment with life after death, but when they're in the temporary state of death, their past sins literally come back to haunt them. Kiefer Sutherland's past sin was a lot scarier than Kevin Bacon's; it's too bad those weren't switched around. When he was young, Kiefer Sutherland had accidentally killed a kid, and the kid kept coming back and terrorizing him.

1991   Queens Logic

None of us has seen *Queens Logic,* which Kevin Bacon was in, but it sounds like it could be good.

The crazy premise for *Pyrates* can't belittle the fact that Kevin acted in this one with his wife, Kyra Sedgwick. The other 1991 movie he acted in is *JFK,* an amazing movie. He

1991   Pyrates

1991   JFK

plays Willie O'Keefe, who's in jail. There's a crazy scene where he's actually dressed as Marie Antoinette, in Joe Pesci's flashback. (Joe Pesci wears a blond wig in this movie, by the way.) Gary Oldman is also in *JFK,* another great reason to see the movie (he plays Lee Harvey Oswald).

There are a lot of spectacular actors in *JFK,* which is why we generally try to stay away from it while playing the game. It's just too easy. But sometimes you're there, and you might as well hit it. When we first started the game, before we'd narrowed it down to six degrees, we used to go through as many cool movies as possible and then wind up with, say, *Diner.* Keeping it down to six steps, you don't always have that luxury.

1991   *He Said, She Said*

He Said, She Said delivers another great performance. He's crazy for not getting back together with his ex-girlfriend in that movie (played by Sharon Stone).

1992   *A Few Good Men*

Kevin Bacon's a tough character to root for in *A Few Good Men,* where he's the opposing counsel, but he's basically a good guy. He's still a friend, underneath it all. There is one major point that Tom Cruise is wrong about—when he walks out of the bar and says to Kevin, "And by the way, you're a lousy softball player!" Kevin Bacon would be a great softball player. He'd be a good shortstop, or maybe he's a little tall for that, but he'd definitely be a good center fielder. Anyone who can ride a bicycle like he did in *Quicksilver* can *not* be a lousy softball player. In *Footloose,* he's jumping and flipping around like Nadia Comaneci through the fields of Utah, and they call him a lousy softball player?

1994   *The River Wild*

In *The River Wild* he's a psychopath again. This is the third time he's been a psychopath. They'd tried this same concept in *White Water Summer*—put Kevin Bacon on the water and make him a psychopath—but the movie had two titles and it bombed. So they gave it another shot, and in *Criminal Law* they made him a bad guy in an urban setting. That got a response, and they decided to put him back on the water.

Next in 1994 he's in *The Air Up There,* which we've never

seen. We really should check it out, because that was the movie that was playing in theaters when we invented this game. But we all saw *Murder in the First,* which is probably

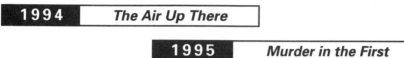

1994   *The Air Up There*

1995   *Murder in the First*

his best performance to date. The first amazing thing about it is that he's playing someone in his twenties. The second amazing thing is that he lost twenty pounds for the role. So even though he didn't show much athletic skill during the film, he performed a lot of athletics to lose the weight to be in it. And it was amazing how quickly and efficiently he killed that guy with the spoon.

   Apollo 13 is another great movie. He plays Jack Swigert. You've heard of Buzz Aldrin and Neil Armstrong, but who's ever heard of Jack Swigert? You'd think they'd at least make Kevin the number two guy. On the other hand, Bill

1995   *Balto*

1995   *Apollo 13*

Paxton is sick all the time, so it's good that he didn't have that character.

1996   *Sleepers*

Six Degrees of Kevin Bacon will only get better. Kevin's got a long and wonderful career in front of him, and the game will expand with him. We're looking forward to playing it for a long time to come.

PART ONE

THE
Basic Bacon

MISSING LINKS

Start with some basic connections, just to get warmed up. One person fits between each of these people and Kevin Bacon.

1. Lisa Bonet

Kevin Bacon

2. Patricia Arquette

Kevin Bacon

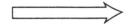

3. Rodney Dangerfield

Kevin Bacon

4. Martin Landau

Kevin Bacon

KEVINS TO KEVIN

Kevin Costner   was in *JFK* with Kevin Bacon

. . . a direct link

There must be some more Kevins out there, but these are the people we could come up with. Give us a Kevin, we'll get him to Kevin.

5. Kevin Kline

6. Kevin Pollak

7. Kevin Spacey

8. Kevin Dillon

THE BALDWIN FAMILY TREE

This is probably not how the Baldwin brothers envision their family tree, but . . .

BILLY

was in *Flatliners* with

STEPHEN

was in *Threesome*
with Laura Flynn Boyle

who was in *The Temp*
with Timothy Hutton

DANIEL

was in *Attack of the
50 Ft. Woman* with
Daryl Hannah

ALEC

was in *She's
Having a
Baby* with

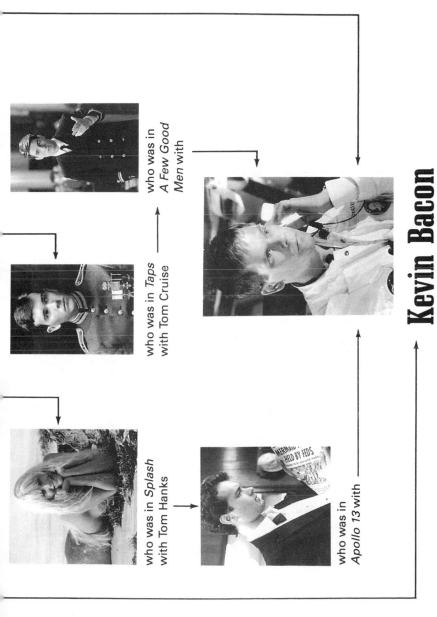

who was in
A Few Good Men with

who was in *Taps*
with Tom Cruise

who was in *Splash*
with Tom Hanks

who was in
Apollo 13 with

Kevin Bacon

BRIDGES TO BACON

When connecting whole families to Kevin Bacon, it's preferable to use different movies for each family member.

9. Lloyd

10. Jeff

11. Beau

MEATHEADS AND BACON

Arnold Schwarzenegger

went to Mars with Sharon
Stone in *Total Recall*

and Sharon Stone was in
He Said, She Said with
Kevin Bacon.

12. Jean-Claude Van Damme

13. Lou Ferrigno

14. Hulk Hogan

15. Steven Seagal

16. Sylvester Stallone

Okay, if you can do Sly, you can obviously do these next two, because they were in the *Rocky* movies. The real aficianado, though, will avoid the *Rocky* route and still get back to Bacon.

17. Mr. T

18. Dolph Lundgren

BACON AND LEGS

Julia Roberts connects to Kevin Bacon in one step: *Flatliners*.

19. Tina Turner

20. Kathy Ireland

21. Cindy Crawford

22. Iman

23. Christine Brinkley

24. Elle MacPherson

25. Paulina Porizkova

SINGING TO BACON

Everyone always wants to know how to connect Elvis to Bacon. Here's *our* answer:

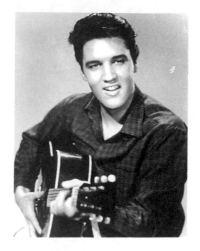

Elvis

was in *Clambake* with Bill Bixby

who was in *The Kentucky Fried Movie* with Donald Sutherland

who was in *Animal House* with Kevin Bacon

26. Madonna

27. Harry Connick, Jr.

28. Eddie Vedder

29. Sting

30. Bette Midler

31. Barbra Streisand

32. Sammy Davis, Jr.

33. The Monkees

34. Dolly Parton

RAPPING TO BACON

Will Smith

was in *Independence Day* with Judd Hirsch

who was in *Ordinary People* with Elizabeth McGovern

who was in *She's Having a Baby* with
Kevin Bacon

35. Ice-T

36. Ice Cube

37. Vanilla Ice

38. Queen Latifah

39. Marky Mark

40. The Fat Boys

41. LL Cool J

42. Tone Lōc

We usually play Six Degrees of Kevin Bacon with recent films, but it's important to prove that the Six Degrees holds true for everyone in the movie universe. Not to spend too much time on this, here're some hints in case you want your grandparents to play.

Check out the older actors who appear in Kevin Bacon's movies.

For instance, in *JFK* you have

Walter Matthau

Ed Asner

and Jack Lemmon.

In *The Big Picture* you have

Eddie Albert

and June Lockhart.

So, if you're into old movies, you just have to get to one of these people in five steps.

For Instance, here's one we got from our parents:

Ronald Reagan

was in *An Angel from Texas* with Eddie Albert

who was in *The Big Picture* with Kevin Bacon

Also, you should think of old movies with huge casts, like *It's a Mad, Mad, Mad, Mad World* (which even has Buster Keaton in it) or *Murder by Death*.

PART TWO

Television

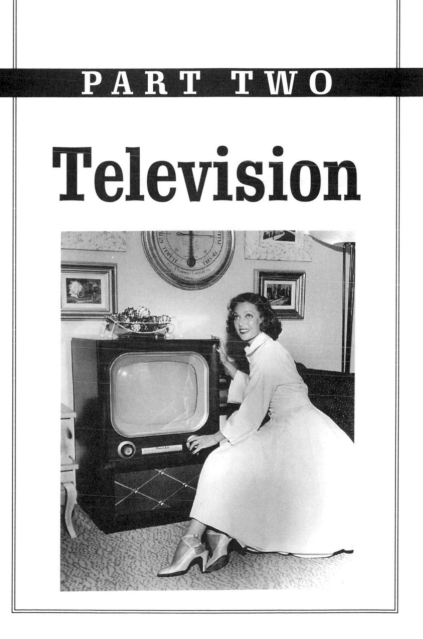

OUR RULES

At first we didn't consider television when linking people up to Kevin Bacon. But eventually we gave in. So many people asked us to do television stars that we just started doing them.

We do have a few ground rules. Cameos on television shows don't count. For a series show, only regularly appearing actors can be used. For a made-for-TV-movie, it has to be a real part, not a few seconds on screen.

Anyway, those are the rules we use.

You can get everyone on Jerry's show to Kevin Bacon, no problem.

43. Elaine

44. George

45. Kramer

46. Newman

THE FACTS OF LIFE

We had to cry uncle when it came to Lisa Whelchel and Mindy Cohen. Hey, you have to save a few people for *Six Degrees of Kevin Bacon II*. As for the rest of the cast, they definitely connect to Kevin Bacon.

47. Nancy McKeon

48. Kim Fields

49. Charlotte Rae

50. George Clooney

A long and distinguished list . . .

51. David Letterman

52. Richard Dawson

53. Bob Barker

54. Arsenio Hall

55. Rosie O'Donnell

56. Ricki Lake

57. Greg Kinnear

58. Joan Rivers

PART THREE

THE
Unusual Bacon

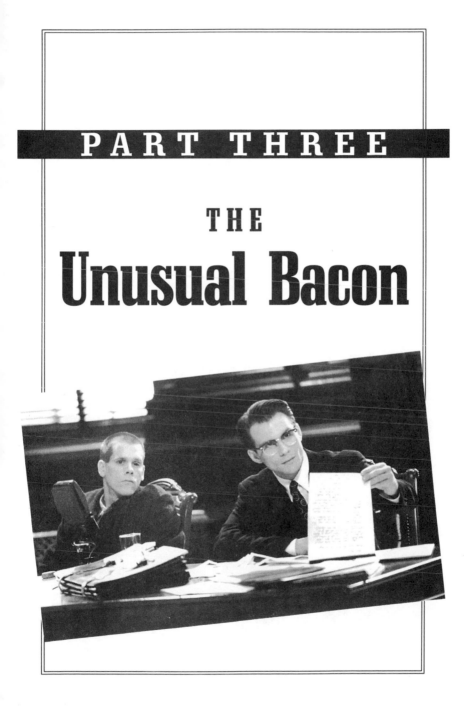

DANCING TO *FOOTLOOSE*

Here's a challenge. Get each of these dancing stars to Kevin Bacon

. . . through Footloose.

59. Jennifer Beals

60. Mikhail Baryshnikov

61. Patrick Swayze

62. John Travolta

63. Boogaloo Shrimp

64. Shabba-Doo

PIGSKINS TO BACON

O. J. Simpson

was in *Capricorn One*
with Elliott Gould

who was in *The Big
Picture* with Kevin Bacon

Yet another long and distinguished list . . .

65. Dan Marino

66. Joe Theismann

67. Jim Brown

68. Bubba Smith

69. Roger Craig

70. Brian Bosworth

THE ANIMAL KINGDOM

Beethoven

was in *Beethoven* with Charles Grodin

who was in *Midnight Run* with Robert De Niro

who was in *Heat* with Val Kilmer,
who was in *Tombstone* with Bill Paxton

. . . who was in *Apollo 13*
with Kevin Bacon

71. Lassie (old)

72. Lassie (new)

73. Cujo

74. Silver

75. Flipper

76. Jaws

BRINGING HOME THE BACON

Pig actors. Sort of a subset of the Animal Kingdom . . . sort of a class in itself.

77. Miss Piggy

78. Babe

79. The singing pigs from *Mary Poppins*

80. Wilbur

SUPERBACON

Superman (see previous page) was in *Superman* with

Gene Hackman

who was in *Mississippi Burning* with Willem Dafoe

who was in *Platoon* with Johnny Depp

who was in *Benny & Joon* with Oliver Platt

who was in *Flatliners* with Kevin Bacon

81. Supergirl   **83.** Blankman

82. The Phantom   **84.** RoboCop

85. The Greatest American Hero

CLOSE ENCOUNTERS WITH KEVIN

These aliens bring Kevin Bacon within six degrees of, basically, the entire universe.

86. Yoda

87. E.T.

88. *Independence Day*'s aliens

89. Predator

90. Klingon

91. *Alien*'s alien

92. *Close Encounters*' aliens

93. *Earth Girls Are Easy*'s aliens

94. **batteries not included*'s aliens

DRIVING MR. BACON

The Millennium Falcon

was in *Star Wars* with Carrie Fisher

who was in *The Blues Brothers*
with John Belushi

COLLEGE

who was in *Animal House* with
Kevin Bacon

A tribute to the great movie vehicles . . . and Kit.

95. Herbie

96. Ecto-l

97. The Winnebago from *Spaceballs*

98. U.S.S. Enterprise

99. Rosebud

100. Christine

101. The Red Car

102. Kit

103. Little Nellie

104. Memphis Belle

MONSTERS, NOT INCLUDING THOSE HUGE SAND WORMS FROM *TREMORS*

The Fly is Jeff Goldblum

who was in *The Big Chill* with Kevin Costner (he played the dead guy)

who was in *JFK* with Kevin Bacon

105. The Gremlins

106. Godzilla

107. King Kong

108. The Loch Ness Monster

109. The Blob (old)

110. The Blob (new)

111. Norm the Gnome

DYNAMIC DUOS

Take the *first* person in the pair and get *to* Bacon in six steps or less.

Then, *from* Bacon, go backward to the *second* person in the pair . . . *using entirely different movies.*

113. Sonny and Cher

114. Adam West and Burt Ward

For this one we had to use the movie going one way and the TV show going the other way.

115. Bruce and Brandon Lee

116. Woody and Mia

117. Cheech and Chong

118. Laverne and Shirley

119. Bogart and Bacall

PART FOUR

THE
Answers

These aren't the *only* answers, they may not be the *fastest* answers, they may not even be *your* answers—but they're the answers that we like the best.

Part I

MISSING LINKS

1. Mickey Rourke connects these two. He's with Lisa Bonet in *Angel Heart,* and he's in *Diner* with Kevin Bacon.

2. Bronson Pinchot was with Patricia Arquette in *True Romance,* and he's in *The Big Picture* with Kevin Bacon.

3. Tommy Lee Jones was in *Natural Born Killers* with Rodney Dangerfield, and he's in *JFK* with Kevin Bacon.

4. Sarah Jessica Parker was in *Ed Wood* with Martin Landau, and she's in *Footloose* with Kevin Bacon.

KEVINS TO KEVIN

5. Kevin Kline

was in *A Fish Called Wanda* with John Cleese
who was in *The Big Picture* with Kevin Bacon

6. Kevin Pollak

was in *A Few Good Men* with Kevin Bacon

7. Kevin Spacey

was in *The Usual Suspects* with Chazz Palminteri
who was in *Bullets Over Broadway* with Diane Wiest
who was in *Footloose* with Kevin Bacon

8. Kevin Dillon

was in *No Escape* with Ray Liotta
who was in *GoodFellas* with Joe Pesci
who was in *JFK* with Kevin Bacon

BRIDGES TO BACON

9. Lloyd

was in *Blown Away* with Tommy Lee Jones
who was in *JFK* with Kevin Bacon

10. Jeff

was in *Fearless* with Rosie Perez
who was in *White Men Can't Jump* with Woody Harrelson
who was in *Indecent Proposal* with Demi Moore
who was in *A Few Good Men* with Kevin Bacon

11. Beau

was in *The Positively True Adventures of the Alleged Texas
Cheerleader-Murdering Mom* with Holly Hunter
who was in *Raising Arizona* with Randall "Tex" Cobb

who was in *Fletch Lives* with Chevy Chase
who was in *L.A. Story* with Sarah Jessica Parker
who was in *Footloose* with Kevin Bacon

MEATHEADS AND BACON

12. Jean-Claude Van Damme

was in *Timecop* with Mia Sara
who was in *Ferris Bueller's Day Off* with Matthew Broderick
who was in *The Freshman* with Bruno Kirby
who was in *City Slickers* with Daniel Stern
who was in *Diner* with Kevin Bacon

13. Lou Ferrigno

was in *The Trial of the Incredible Hulk* with Bill Bixby
who was in *Kentucky Fried Movie* with Donald Sutherland
   (directed by John Landis, who puts the line "See you next
   Wednesday" in every one of his movies)
who was in *Animal House* with Kevin Bacon

14. Hulk Hogan

was in *Suburban Commando* with Christopher Lloyd
who was in *Back to Future II* with Elisabeth Shue
who was in *Heart and Souls* with Kyra Sedgwick
who was in *Pyrates* with Kevin Bacon

15. Steven Seagal

was in *Hard to Kill* with Kelly LeBrock
who was in *Weird Science* with Anthony Michael Hall
who was in *Six Degrees of Separation* with Donald Sutherland
   (our hats are off to this movie)
who was in *JFK* with Kevin Bacon

16. Sylvester Stallone

was in *The Specialist* with Sharon Stone
who was in *He Said, She Said* with Kevin Bacon

Sure, it's easy to go the Sly route on the next two, but check these out:

17. Mr. T

was in *DC Cab* with Paul Rodriguez
who was in *Quicksilver* with Kevin Bacon

18. Dolph Lundgren

was in *The Punisher* with Lou Gosset, Jr.
who was in *An Officer and a Gentleman* with Richard Gere
who was in *Pretty Woman* with Julia Roberts
who was in *Flatliners* with Kevin Bacon

BACON AND LEGS

The idea for this chapter came from Mrs. Ginelli, by the way.

19. Tina Turner

was in *Mad Max Beyond Thunderdome* with Mel Gibson
who was in *Lethan Weapon 2* with Joe Pesci
who was in *JFK* with Kevin Bacon

20. Kathy Ireland

was in *Loaded Weapon I* with Whoopi Goldberg
who was in *Made in America* with Ted Danson
who was in *3 Men and a Baby* with Steve Guttenberg
who was in *Diner* with Kevin Bacon

21. Cindy Crawford

was in *Pret-a-Porter* with Tim Robbins
who was in *The Shawshank Redemption* with Morgan Freeman
who was in *Outbreak* with Cuba Gooding, Jr.

who was in *A Few Good Men* with Kevin Bacon

22. Iman

was in *L.A. Story* with Sarah Jessica Parker
who was in *Footloose* with Kevin Bacon

23. Christine Brinkley

was in *Vacation* with Randy Quaid
who was in *Independence Day* with Brent Spiner
who was in *Phenomenon* with Kyra Sedgwick
who was in *Murder in the First* with Kevin Bacon

24. Elle MacPherson

was in *Sirens* with Hugh Grant
who was in *Four Weddings and a Funeral* with Andie McDowell
who was in *Bad Girls* with Mary Stuart Masterson
who was in *At Close Range* with Kiefer Sutherland
who was in *Flatliners* with Kevin Bacon

25. Paulina Porizkova

was in *Her Alibi* with Tom Selleck
who was in *3 Men and a Baby* with Steve Guttenberg
who was in *Diner* with Kevin Bacon

26. Madonna

was in *Desperately Seeking Susan* with Aidan Quinn
who was in *Benny & Joon* with Oliver Platt
who was in *Flatliners* with Kevin Bacon

27. Harry Connick, Jr.

was in *Copycat* with Holly Hunter
who was in *The Piano* with Harvey Keitel
who was in *Reservoir Dogs* with Christopher Penn
who was in *Footloose* with Kevin Bacon

28. Eddie Vedder

was in *Singles* with Kyra Sedgwick
who was in *Pyrates* with Kevin Bacon

29. Sting

was in *Dune* with Virginia Madsen
who was in *Thelma and Louise* with Susan Sarandon
who was in *Bull Durham* with Kevin Costner
who was in *JFK* with Kevin Bacon

30. Bette Midler

was in *Outrageous Fortune* with Shelley Long
who was in *The Money Pit* with Tom Hanks
who was in *Apollo 13* with Kevin Bacon

31. Sammy Davis, Jr.

was in *Cannonball Run* with Jamie Farr
who was in *Speed Zone* with John Candy
who was in *Planes, Trains & Automobiles* with Kevin Bacon

32. Barbra Streisand

was in *Nuts* with Richard Dreyfuss
who was in *Moon Over Parador* with Raul Julia
who was in *The Addams Family* with Christina Ricci
who was in *Now and Then* with Demi Moore

who was in *A Few Good Men* with Kevin Bacon

33. The Monkees

They were in *The Brady Bunch Movie* with Shelley Long
who was in *Outrageous Fortune* with Peter Coyote
who was in *Jagged Edge* with Glenn Close
who was in *House of Spirits* with Meryl Streep
who was in *The River Wild* with Kevin Bacon

34. Dolly Parton

was in *The Best Little Whorehouse in Texas* with Burt Reynolds
who was in *Striptease* with Demi Moore
who was in *A Few Good Men* with Kevin Bacon

RAPPING TO BACON

35. Ice-T

was in *New Jack City* with Judd Nelson
who was in *The Breakfast Club* with Emilio Estevez
who was in *Young Guns* with Kiefer Sutherland
who was in *Flatliners* with Kevin Bacon

36. Ice Cube

was in *Boyz N the Hood* with Laurence Fishburne
who was in *Quicksilver* with Kevin Bacon

37. Vanilla Ice

was in *Cool as Ice* with Michael Gross
who was in *Tremors* with Kevin Bacon

38. Queen Latifah

was in *My Life* with Michael Keaton
who was in *Batman* with Kim Basinger
who was in *The Getaway* with Alec Baldwin
who was in *She's Having a Baby* with Kevin Bacon

39. Marky Mark

was in *The Basketball Diaries* with Leonard DiCaprio
who was with Sharon Stone in *The Quick and the Dead*
who was with Kevin Bacon in *He Said, She Said*

40. The Fat Boys

were in *Disorderlies* with Ralph Bellamy
who was in *Cocoon* with Steve Guttenberg

who was in *Diner* with Kevin Bacon

104

41. LL Cool J

was in *Toys* with Robin Williams
who was in *The World According to Garp* with John Lithgow
who was in *Footloose* with Kevin Bacon

42. Tone Lōc

was in *The Adventures of Ford Fairlane* with Gilbert Gottfried
who was in *Beverly Hills Cop II* with Paul Reiser
who was in *Diner* with Kevin Bacon

Part II: Television

SEINFELD

43. Elaine

Julia Louis-Dreyfus was in *Christmas Vacation* with Randy
  Quaid
who was in *Major League II* with Tom Berenger
who was in *Shattered* with Greta Scacchi
who was in *Presumed Innocent* with Harrison Ford
who was in *Raiders of the Lost Ark* with Karen Allen
who was in *Animal House* with Kevin Bacon

44. George

Jason Alexander was in *The Paper* with Glenn Close
who was in *The Natural* with Wilford Brimley
who was in *The Firm* with David Strathairn
who was in *The River Wild* with Kevin Bacon

45. Kramer

Michael Richards was in *So I Married an Axe Murderer* with
  Michael Myers

who was in *Wayne's World II* with Drew Barrymore
who was in *Poison Ivy* with Tom Skerritt
who was in *Top Gun* with Tom Cruise
who was in *A Few Good Men* with Kevin Bacon

46. Newman

was in *Jurassic Park* with Laura Dern
who was in *Wild at Heart* with Willem Dafoe
who was in *Mississippi Burning* with Lee Ermey
who was in *Murder in the First* with Kevin Bacon

THE FACTS OF LIFE

Once again, our apologies to Lisa Whelchel and Mindy Cohen.

47. Nancy McKeon

was in *Where the Day Takes You* with Christian Slater
who was in *Murder in the First* with Kevin Bacon

48. Kim Fields

was in *Living Single* with Queen Latifah
who was in *My Life* with Michael Keaton
who was in *Batman* with Jack Nicholson
who was in *A Few Good Men* with Kevin Bacon

49. Charlotte Rae

was in *Different Strokes* with Gary Coleman
who was in *The Kid with the Broken Halo* with Robert Guillame
who was in *Soap* with Billy Crystal
who was in *City Slickers* with Daniel Stern
who was in *Diner* with Kevin Bacon

50. George Clooney

was in *Dusk Till Dawn* with Quentin Tarantino
who was in *Sleep With Me* with Eric Stoltz
who was in *Singles* with Kyra Sedgwick

who was in *Pyrates* with Kevin Bacon

TV HOSTS

51. David Letterman

was with Chris Elliott in *Cabin Boy*
who was in *The Abyss*—you know, it's such a serious movie,
   and then right at the climax, they're raising the ship out of
   the water, and Chris Elliott shows up out of *nowhere,* and it
   completely ruins the mood—
anyway, he's in *The Abyss* with Ed Harris
who was in *Apollo 13* with Kevin Bacon

52. Richard Dawson

was in *Running Man* with Arnold Schwarzenegger
who was in *Junior* with Danny DeVito
who was in *Tin Men* with Barbara Hershey
who was in *Hannah and Her Sisters* with Dianne Wiest
who was in *Footloose* with Kevin Bacon

53. Bob Barker

was in *Happy Gilmore* with Adam Sandler
who was in *Mixed Nuts* with Rita Wilson

who was in *Bonfire of the Vanities* with Tom Hanks
who was in *Apollo 13* with Kevin Bacon

54. Arsenio Hall

was in *Coming to America* with Louis Anderson
who was in *Quicksilver* with Kevin Bacon

55. Rosie O'Donnell

was in *Sleepless in Seattle* with Rob Reiner
who was in *This Is Spinal Tap* with Christopher Guest
who was in *A Few Good Men* with Kevin Bacon

56. Ricki Lake

was in *Serial Mom* with Kathleen Turner
who was in *The Man with Two Brains* with Steve Martin
who was in *Father of the Bride* with Martin Short
who was in *The Big Picture* with Kevin Bacon

57. Greg Kinnear

was in *Sabrina* with Lauren Holly
who was in *Beautiful Girls* with Matt Dillon
who was in *Singles* with Kyra Sedgwick
who was in *Pyrates* with Kevin Bacon

58. Joan Rivers

Even though she's just a voice, we had to put her in here.

She was in *Spaceballs* with Bill Pullman
who was in *The Favor* with Elizabeth McGovern
who was in *She's Having a Baby* with Kevin Bacon

Part III: The Unusual Bacon

59. Jennifer Beals

> from *Flashdance,* of course; she was also in *Dorothy Parker and the Vicious Circle* with Andrew McCarthy
> who was in *Less Than Zero* with Robert Downey, Jr.
> who was in *The Pick-Up Artist* with Harvey Keitel
> who was in *Reservoir Dogs* with Christopher Penn
> who was in *Footloose* with Kevin Bacon

60. Mikhail Baryshnikov

who was in *White Nights* with Isabella Rossellini
who was in *Death Becomes Her* with Bruce Willis
who was in *Striking Distance* with Sarah Jessica Parker
who was in *Footloose* with Kevin Bacon

61. Patrick Swayze

who was in *Dirty Dancing* with Jennifer Grey
who was in *Ferris Bueller's Day Off* with Matthew Broderick
who was in *The Road to Wellville* with John Cusack
who was in *Bullets Over Broadway* with Dianne Wiest
who was in *Footloose* with Kevin Bacon

62. John Travolta

was in *Urban Cowboy* with Debra Winger
who was in *Terms of Endearment* with John Lithgow
who was in *Footloose* with Kevin Bacon

63. Boogaloo Shrimp

Michael Chambers was in *Naked Gun 33⅓* with Priscilla Presley
who was in *The Adventures of Ford Fairlane* with Robert
  Englund
who was in *A Nightmare on Elm Street* with Johnny Depp
who was in *Edward Scissorhands* with Diane Wiest
who was in *Footloose* with Kevin Bacon

64. Shabba-Doo

Adolfo Quinones was in *Tango and Cash* with Sylvester
  Stallone
who was in *Cliffhanger* with John Lithgow
who was in *Footloose* with Kevin Bacon

65. Dan Marino

was in *Ace Ventura, Pet Detective* with Sean Young
who was in *Fatal Instinct* with Bob Uecker
who was in *Major League* with Charlie Sheen
who was in *Young Guns* with Kiefer Sutherland
who was in *Flatliners* with Kevin Bacon

66. Joe Theisman

was in *Cannonball Run II* with Tony Danza
who was in *Going Ape!* with Danny DeVito
who was in *Twins* with Arnold Schwarzenegger
who was in *Last Action Hero* with Sharon Stone
who was in *He Said, She Said* with Kevin Bacon

67. Jim Brown

was in *The Dirty Dozen* with Donald Sutherland
who was in *Animal House* with Kevin Bacon

68. Bubba Smith

was in *Police Academy* with Steve Guttenberg
who was in *Diner* with Kevin Bacon

69. Roger Craig

was in *Necessary Roughness* with Darryl Cox
who was in *JFK* with Kevin Bacon

70. Brian Bosworth

was in *Stone Cold* with William Forsythe
who was in *Once Upon a Time in America* with Jennifer
    Connelly
who was in *Higher Learning* with Kristi Swanson
who was in *Buffy, the Vampire Slayer* with Donald Sutherland
who was in *Animal House* with Kevin Bacon

71. Lassie (old)

was with Elizabeth Taylor
who was in *The Flintstones* with Elizabeth Perkins
who was in *He Said, She Said* with Kevin Bacon

72. Lassie (new)

was with Helen Slater
who was in *The Legend of Billie Jean* with Christian Slater
who was in *Murder in the First* with Kevin Bacon

73. Cujo

was with Danny Pintauro
who was in *The Beniker Gang* with J. T. Walsh
who was in *A Few Good Men* with Kevin Bacon

74. Silver

was in the *The Legend of the Lone Ranger* with Jason Robards
who was in *Philadelphia* with Tom Hanks
who was in *Apollo 13* with Kevin Bacon

75. Flipper

Flipper acted with Elijah Wood
who was in *The War* with Kevin Costner
who was in *JFK* with Kevin Bacon

76. Jaws

The best route of many is to use Roy Scheider
who was in *Blue Thunder* with Daniel Stern
who was in *Diner* with Kevin Bacon

77. Miss Piggy

was in *The Great Muppet Caper* with Charles Grodin
who was in *Midnight Run* (great movie) with Robert De Niro
who was in *Taxi Driver* with Albert Brooks
who was in *Defending Your Life* with Meryl Streep
who was in *The River Wild* with Kevin Bacon

78. Babe

Farmer Hoggett was played by James Cromwell
who was in *Murder by Death* (he's James Coco's assistant)
  with Peter Falk
who was in *The Princess Bride* with Robin Wright
who was in *Forrest Gump* with Tom Hanks
who was in *Apollo 13* with Kevin Bacon

79. The singing pigs from *Mary Poppins*

was with Julie Andrews

who was in *Victor/Victoria* with James Garner
who was in *Maverick* with Mel Gibson
who was in *Lethal Weapon 3* with Joe Pesci
who was in *JFK* with Kevin Bacon

80. Wilbur

From *Charlotte's Web:*
Charlotte is played by Debbie Reynolds
who is in *The Bodyguard* with Kevin Costner
who is in *JFK* with Kevin Bacon

SUPERBACON

81. Supergirl

is Helen Slater, who was in *Ruthless People* with Judge
   Reinhold
who was in *Vice Versa* with Fred Savage
who was in *The Princess Bride* with Billy Crystal
who was in *City Slickers* with Daniel Stern
who was in *Diner* with Kevin Bacon

82. The Phantom

is Billy Zane, who was in *Dead Calm* with Nicole Kidman
who was in *Malice* with Alec Baldwin
who was in *She's Having a Baby* with Kevin Bacon

83. Blankman

is Damon Wayans, who acted in *Blankman* with Halle Berre
who was in *Losing Isaiah* with David Strathairn

who was in *The River Wild* with Kevin Bacon

---

84. RoboCop

was played by Peter Weller, who was in *Buckaroo Banzai* (the full title of that movie being *The Adventures of Buckaroo Banzai Across the Eighth Dimension*) with Ellen Barkin who was in *Diner* with Kevin Bacon

85. The Greatest American Hero

was William Katt, who was in *House* with Norm (George Wendt)
who was in *Kazaam* with Shaquille O'Neal
who was in *Blue Chips* with Nick Nolte
who was in *I Love Trouble* with Julia Roberts
who was in *Flatliners* with Kevin Bacon

CLOSE ENCOUNTERS WITH KEVIN

86. Yoda

was in *Empire Strikes Back* with Harrison Ford
who was in *Raiders of the Lost Ark* with Karen Allen
who was in *Animal House* with Kevin Bacon

87. E.T.

was with Henry Thomas
who was in *Legends of the Fall* with Brad Pitt
who was in *True Romance* with Gary Oldman
who was in *Criminal Law* with Kevin Bacon

88. *Independence Day*'s aliens

President Bill Pullman was in *Sleepless in Seattle* with Tom Hanks
who was in *Apollo 13* with Kevin Bacon

89. Predator

(probably the greatest alien of the bunch) was in the jungle with Arnold Schwarzenegger
who was in *Total Recall* with Sharon Stone
who was in *He Said, She Said* with Kevin Bacon

90. Klingon

The original Klingon was Christopher Lloyd
who was in *The Dream Team* with Stephen Furst
who was in *Animal House* with Kevin Bacon

91. *Alien's* alien

Sigourney Weaver, obviously
who was in *Working Girl* with Joan Cusack
who was in *Sixteen Candles* with Jami Gertz

who was *Quicksilver* with Kevin Bacon

92. *Close Encounters'* aliens

There are a lot of easy ways to get there, but we like to use
    Richard Dreyfuss
who was in *Down and Out in Beverly Hills* with Nick Nolte
who was in *48 HRS.* with Eddie Murphy
who was in *Beverly Hills Cop* with Paul Reiser
who was in *Diner* with Kevin Bacon

93. *Earth Girls Are Easy*'s aliens

Julie Brown was in *The Opposite Sex and How to Live with Them* with Kevin Pollak
who was in *A Few Good Men* with Kevin Bacon

94. **batteries not included*'s aliens

were with Jessica Tandy
who was in *Cocoon* with Steve Guttenberg
who was in *Diner* with Kevin Bacon

DRIVING MR. BACON

95. Herbie

The Love Bug was with Don Knotts,
who was in *Cannonball Run II* with Shirley MacLaine
who was in *Steel Magnolias* with Daryl Hannah
who was in *Roxanne* with Steve Martin
who was in *Planes, Trains & Automobiles* with Kevin Bacon

96. Ecto-I

was the car in *Ghostbusters* with Rick Moranis
who was in *My Blue Heaven* with Steve Martin
who was in *Planes, Trains & Automobiles* with Kevin Bacon

97. The Winnebago from *Spaceballs*

was with John Candy
who was also in *Planes, Trains & Automobiles* with Kevin Bacon

98. U.S.S. Enterprise

was in *Star Trek Generations* with Malcolm McDowell
who was in *Tank Girl* with Lori Petty
who was in *Point Break* with Keanu Reeves
who was in *Parenthood* with Steve Martin
who was in *Planes, Trains & Automobiles* with Kevin Bacon

99. Rosebud

from *Citizen Kane,* with Orson Welles
who was in *The Muppet Movie* with Steve Martin
who was in *Planes, Trains & Automobiles* with Kevin Bacon

100. Christine

A '58 Plymouth, by the way.

Keith Gordon owns Christine
and he's in *The Legend of Billie Jean* with Christian Slater
who was in *Murder in the First* with Kevin Bacon

101. The Red Car

from *Who Framed Roger Rabbit?* with Bob Hoskins
   (Christopher Lloyd buys out the Red Car in order to build a
   freeway)
who was in *Hook* with Julia Roberts
who was in *Flatliners* with Kevin Bacon

102. Kit

was the car in *Knight Rider* with David Hasselhoff
who was in *Baywatch* with Nicole Eggart
who was in *Blown Away* with Cory Feldman (one of the many
   movies with the two Corys in it—the other Cory being Cory
   Haim)
who was in *The Goonies* with Shawn Astin
who was in *White Water Summer* with Kevin Bacon

103. Little Nellie

Low blow, but that's the name of the helicopter in *You Only
   Live Twice,* with Sean Connery
who was in *Just Cause* with Laurence Fishburne
who was in *Quicksilver* with Kevin Bacon

104. Memphis Belle

was flown by Matthew Modine
who was in *Full Metal Jacket* with Lee Ermey
who was in *Murder in the First* with Kevin Bacon

105. The Gremlins

were in *Gremlins* with Phoebe Cates
who was in *Fast Times at Ridgemont High* with Jennifer Jason Leigh
who was in *The Big Picture* with Kevin Bacon

106. Godzilla

appeared in *Blazing Saddles* with Gene Wilder
who was in *Stir Crazy* with Richard Pryor
who was in *Brewster's Millions* with John Candy
who was in *Planes, Trains & Automobiles* with Kevin Bacon

107. King Kong

Jessica Lange is in *King Kong*
and she won that Oscar for *Blue Sky* with Tommy Lee Jones
who was in *JFK* with Kevin Bacon

A better way to get there is through Jeff Bridges,
who is in *Blown Away* with Lloyd Bridges,
who is in *Hot Shots* with Charlie Sheen
who is in *Young Guns* with Kiefer Sutherland
who is in *Flatliners* with Kevin Bacon

108. The Loch Ness Monster

was in *Amazon Women on the Moon* with Steve Guttenberg
who was in *Diner* with Kevin Bacon

109. The Blob (old)

was in *The Blob* with Steve McQueen
who was in *Papillon* with Dustin Hoffman
who was in *Rain Man* with Tom Cruise
who was in *A Few Good Men* with Kevin Bacon

110. The Blob (new)

was in *The Blob* with Kevin Dillon
who was in *The Doors* with Val Kilmer
who was in *True Romance* with Gary Oldman
who was in *Murder in the First* with Kevin Bacon

111. Norm the Gnome

was in *A Gnome Named Norm* with Anthony Michael Hall
who was in *Edward Scissorhands* with Winona Ryder
who was in *Dracula* with Gary Oldman
who was in *Criminal Law* with Kevin Bacon

DYNAMIC DUOS

112. Sonny and Cher

Sonny was in *Airplane II* with William Shatner
who was in *Star Trek II* with Kirstie Alley
who was in *Look Who's Talking Too* with John Travolta
who was in *Boris and Natasha* with John Candy
who was in *Planes, Trains & Automobiles* with Kevin Bacon

who was in *A Few Good Men* with Tom Cruise
who was in *The Outsiders* with Patrick Swayze
who was in *Road House* with Sam Elliott
who was in *Mask* with Cher

113. Adam West and Burt Ward

Adam West was in *Batman* (the movie) with Burgess Meredith
who was in *Rocky* with Sylvester Stallone
who was in *Cliffhanger* with John Lithgow
who was in *Footloose* with Kevin Bacon

who was in *He Said, She Said* with Elizabeth Perkins
who was in *The Flintstones* with Halle Berre
who was in *Boomerang* with Eartha Kitt

who was in *Batman* (the TV show) with Burt Ward

114. Bruce and Brandon Lee

Bruce Lee was in Game of Death with Kareem Abdul-Jabbar
   (Kareem's debut!)
who was in *Airplane* with Leslie Nielsen
who was in *Naked Gun 33⅓* with Elliott Gould
who was in *The Big Picture* with Kevin Bacon

who was in *JFK* with Kevin Costner
who was in *Robin Hood: Prince of Thieves* with Alan Rickman
who was *The Crow* with Brandon Lee

115. Woody and Mia

Woody Allen was in *Mighty Aphrodite* with Michael Rapaport
who was in *Parenthood* with Dianne Wiest
who was in *Footloose* with Kevin Bacon

who was in *A Few Good Men* with Demi Moore
who was in *Indecent Proposal* with Robert Redford
who was in *The Great Gatsby* with Mia Farrow

116. Cheech and Chong

Tough one.

Chong was in *Up In Smoke* with Pee Wee Herman (Paul Reubens)
who was in *Buffy the Vampire Slayer* with Donald Sutherland
who was in *Animal House* with Kevin Bacon

who was in *Quicksilver* with Paul Rodriguez
who was in *Born in East L.A.* with Cheech

117. Laverne and Shirley

Penny Marshall played Myrna on *The Odd Couple.*
Al Molinaro from *The Odd Couple* was also in *Happy Days* with Henry Winkler
who was in *Lords of Flatbush* with Sylvester Stallone
who was in *The Specialist* with Sharon Stone
who was in *He Said, She Said* with Kevin Bacon

who was in *Animal House* with John Belushi
who was in *The Blues Brothers* with Dan Ackroyd
who was in *Ghostbusters* with Bill Murray
who was in *What About Bob* with Richard Dreyfuss
who was in *American Grafitti* with Cindy Williams

118. Bogart and Bacall

Humphrey Bogart was in *Casablanca* with Peter Lorre
who was in *20,000 Leagues Under the Sea* with Kirk Douglas
who was in *Oscar* with Marisa Tomei
who was in *Untamed Heart* with Christian Slater
who was in *Murder in the First* with Kevin Bacon

who was in *Apollo 13* with Bill Paxton
who was in *Heat* with Robert De Niro
who was in *Taxi Driver* with Jodie Foster
who was in *Maverick* with James Garner
who was in *The Fan* with Lauren Bacall

Feel free to send us E-mail: any comments, questions, or better routes to Bacon.

GFT@Freemark.com

PLUME

ANNUAL #1 BESTSELLER

LEONARD MALTIN'S
1997 MOVIE & VIDEO GUIDE

**More than 19,000 entries * 300 new films * Ratings from G to NC-17
* Over 13,000 Video and 5,000 Laserdisc Listings
* Expanded Title Indexes of Stars and Directors**

- The latest summer blockbusters
- The classics of John Ford and Alfred Hitchcock
- The comedies of the Marx Brothers
- This year's Oscar winners
- Family films
- Foreign films
- Exact running times
- Official motion picture code ratings
- Ratings from ★★★★ to **BOMB**
- A concise summary and capsule review of each film

**"INCH FOR INCH, DOLLAR FOR DOLLAR, MALTIN'S BOOK
GIVES YOU THE MOST."—Boston Sunday Herald**

(276810—$19.95)